An Animal Park Keeper

Written by Anne Rooney
Illustrated by Nathalie Ortega

Collins

Harper has a job with animals.

2

park keeper

3

In summer the camel sheds hair.

Harper gathers it up.

Otters cavort in the pool.

Harper feeds fish to them.

Harper checks the owl.

Its talons curl onto her arm.

The goats are high up!

Can Harper coax them down?

It turns dark. The owl hoots.

Harper locks the park.

Animals

After reading

Letters and Sounds: Phase 3

Word count: 59

Focus phonemes: /ee/ /igh/ /oa/ /oo/ /ar/ /ur/ /ow/ /air/ /er/ /or/

Common exception words: the, (on)to, are

Curriculum links: Understanding the World: People and communities, The World

Early learning goals: Reading: use phonic knowledge to decode regular words and read them aloud accurately; demonstrate understanding when talking with others about what they have read

Developing fluency

- Your child may enjoy hearing you read the book. Model fluency and expression.
- Encourage your child to sound talk and then blend the words, e.g. k/ee/p/er **keeper**. It may help to point to each sound as your child reads.
- Then ask your child to reread the sentence to support fluency and understanding.

Phonic practice

- Ask your child to sound talk and blend each of the following words: c/oa/x, c/a/v/or/t, h/oo/t/s, H/ar/p/er.
- How many words can your child think of that rhyme with **park**? (e.g. *dark, spark, bark, lark, hark*)
- Look through the book. What words can your child find with the /ar/ sound in? (*Harper, park, arm, dark*)

Extending vocabulary

- Ask your child:
  - On page 11, Harper tries to coax the goats down. What does the word **coax** mean? (e.g. *encourage, charm, persuade*)
  - In the book the owl **hoots**. Can you describe any other animal noises? (e.g. *baa, moo, woof, bark, roar, growl, yelp, meow, cluck, hiss*)